100 RECIPES

IN NO TIME AT ALL

PRODUCED BY  WITHIN 48 HOURS

ON BEHALF OF

BREAKTHROUGH
BREAST CANCER

BBC BOOKS

Acknowledgements

BREAKTHROUGH Breast Cancer would like to thank BBC Books, BBC Pebble Mill, BBC Radio 2 and *Wake Up to Wogan*, Anthony Blake, BT, Butler & Tanner, Central Despatch, Chloe Cheese, Flying Colours, the Four Seasons Hotel, the Good Housekeeping Institute, Duncan Hamilton, Leith's School of Food & Wine, the Colin Martin School of Sugar, Negs, cars by Niven Ltd, Nonya Kitchen, Oddbins Ltd, Rebecca Roth, Sainsbury's, WH Smith Ltd and anyone else who helped out at the last moment . . .

PUBLISHED BY BBC BOOKS,

A DIVISION OF BBC ENTERPRISES LTD

WOODLANDS, 80 WOOD LANE, LONDON W12 0TT

ISBN 0 563 37133 1

FIRST PUBLISHED 1994

REPRINTED 1994 (SIX TIMES)

RECIPES © INDIVIDUAL CONTRIBUTORS, 1994

COMPILATION © BREAKTHROUGH BREAST CANCER, 1994

PHOTOGRAPHS BY ANTHONY BLAKE

ILLUSTRATIONS BY CHLOE CHEESE

TYPESET BY PHIL BASKERVILLE

DESIGNED BY DESIGN/SECTION

PRINTED AND BOUND IN GREAT BRITAIN BY

BUTLER & TANNER LTD, FROME, SOMERSET

As viewers of *Challenge Anneka* will know, this book was put together at great speed. While every effort has been made to ensure that the recipes it contains are as accurate as possible, please do let BBC Books know if you find any errors when you are making these dishes at home.

Contents

INTRODUCTION

At 8am on Tuesday 9 August 1994 we were given an extraordinary Challenge live on Terry Wogan's daily Radio 2 programme. Our task was to compile and publish a book of easy-to-prepare recipes in just two days.

In those frantic, chaotic 48 hours we received the help of a huge number of generous people. Thousands of viewers, listeners and celebrities sent in a wide range of imaginative recipes and I'm sorry we could include only a fraction. Volunteers tested them at the Good Housekeeping Institute and many individuals and companies donated time and resources to help the production process.

Thank you to you all and to everyone who buys this book. With it, BREAKTHROUGH, the breast cancer charity, hopes to go some way towards achieving its own challenge – raising £15 million to create a dedicated Breast Cancer Research Centre with the ultimate aim of finding a cure to this terrible disease.

I feel confident that BREAKTHROUGH will be successful. In the meantime, happy cooking.

With best wishes,

Anneka Rice

BREAKTHROUGH
BREAST CANCER

This year 15000 women will die of breast cancer in the UK. There is no cure – yet. Believe it or not, scientists don't even know how a healthy breast cell actually works, much less how it turns cancerous and why. But BREAKTHROUGH Breast Cancer is determined to change all that. By bringing together top scientists within a dedicated Breast Cancer Research Centre, BREAKTHROUGH intends to concentrate exclusively on research into this one disease until enough is known and a cure is found. Creating this Centre will cost £15 million.

Thank you for buying this book. All revenue from its first printing of 10000 copies will be donated to BREAKTHROUGH, followed by 10% of the retail price on all subsequent sales. The money raised will go towards BREAKTHROUGH's appeal, taking it one step further towards finding a cure.

If you would like to make a donation or find out more, please call 071 405 5111, or write to BREAKTHROUGH Breast Cancer, PO Box 2JP, London W1A 2JP, making any cheques payable to BREAKTHROUGH Breast Cancer.

BREAKTHROUGH Breast Cancer is a registered charity.

STARTERS

Jackie Alliss's Mushrooms Crème Fraiche

ORGANIZER OF CHARITY GOLF EVENTS

Serves 12

6 tbsp olive oil or sunflower oil	*For the dressing*
150 ml (5 fl oz) dry white wine	150 ml (5 fl oz) crème fraiche
2 red onions, finely chopped	1 tsp Dijon mustard
6 tbsp brandy (optional)	*To serve*
salt	12 iceberg lettuce leaves, to serve
freshly ground black pepper	4 tbsp fresh chives, chopped, to serve
225 g (8 oz) button mushrooms	

Place the oil, white wine, onions, brandy (if using), and salt and pepper in a saucepan. Bring to the boil and then simmer over a low heat for 5 minutes or until the onions are soft and transparent. Add the mushrooms to the pan then cover with a tightly fitting lid and simmer for a further 10 minutes. Remove from the heat and cool the mushrooms and their stock, then refrigerate for at least 12 hours.

Drain the mushrooms and discard the stock. Mix together the crème fraiche and mustard.

To serve, place a whole lettuce leaf on each plate (iceberg leaves are very curly and will hold the mushrooms). Place a few mushrooms inside each lettuce leaf then spoon on the crème fraiche dressing. Sprinkle with the chopped chives and serve.

Simple Salmon Mousse

SUE NICE, SURREY

Serves 4

100 g (4 oz) tin of pink or red salmon	freshly ground black pepper
spring onion, chopped	150 ml (5 fl oz) double cream, whipped
pinch of dill	1 egg white, beaten until stiff
grated rind of lemon or lime	1 sachet unflavoured gelatine
2 tbsp mayonnaise	few leaves of frisée lettuce, to garnish
salt	sprigs of watercress, to garnish

In a food processor, whizz together the salmon, spring onion, dill, lemon rind, mayonnaise, salt and pepper. Transfer the mixture to a mixing bowl. Fold in the cream and beaten egg white. Dissolve the gelatine, following the directions on the packet, and add to the mixture, mixing carefully. Transfer the mixture into a 1 pint mould or 1 lb loaf tin lined with non-stick parchment and leave to set in the fridge. Turn out onto a serving dish and serve with a garnish of frisée lettuce and watercress and some chunky granary bread.

Asparagus Mousse with Chive or Chervil Sauce

ERIC DEBLONDE, EXECUTIVE CHEF, FOUR SEASONS HOTEL, LONDON

Serves 2

6 large asparagus spears	1 tsp cornflour
3 eggs	seasoning
500 ml (17 fl oz) double cream	small bunch of chives or chervil, chopped

Pre-heat the oven to 180°C/350°F/Gas 4. Cook the asparagus in boiling salted water for 8–10 minutes until very soft, and cool. Drain the asparagus, setting aside the water, and trim the tips; keep for decoration. Mash the asparagus and add the eggs, double cream, cornflour, and seasoning. Pass through a sieve and pour into two buttered ramekins. Put enough water in an ovenproof dish to go half way up the sides of the ramekins. Cook for 15–20 minutes in the middle of the oven.

Meanwhile, to make the chive or chervil sauce reduce the reserved cooking liquid for 2–3 minutes over a medium heat. Add cream, reduce for a further 2–3 minutes and add chives or chervil. Cook for a minute and put aside. Remove the dish from the oven and invert ramekins onto two plates. Decorate with the tips of asparagus and serve with the chive or chervil sauce.

John Leslie's Crispy Parma Ham and Melon Salad

TV PRESENTER

Serves 4

1 Galia melon	mixed salad leaves to garnish
6 slices Parma ham	(watercress, lamb's lettuce, etc)
1 tbsp olive oil	vinaigrette dressing

Cut the melon into quarters, scoop out the seeds, and carefully remove the peel. Cut each quarter into four slices lengthways and arrange on plates in a fan.

Arrange one or two salad leaves to cover the base of the fan, and dress with a little vinaigrette. Cut the Parma ham into strips and fry gently in the olive oil for 3 minutes until the edges curl. Arrange on plates and serve.

30-second Starter

ROSY BLOCKLEY, HAMPSHIRE

Serves 4

120 g (4½ oz) packet smoked salmon or smoked trout	2 or 3 slivers of fresh root ginger
	salt
175 ml (6 fl oz) fromage frais	freshly ground black pepper
1 sprig fresh dill, finely chopped	

If using smoked trout, skin the fish and take all the flesh from the bones. Put all the ingredients into a food processor and process. Serve with hot toast, or as a dip.

Prawn and Bacon Paté

SOPHIE WALLIS, LONDON

Serves 4

500 g tub mascarpone or other full-fat soft cheese	juice of ½ lemon
	1 tbsp chopped fresh parsley
20 cooked, peeled prawns, roughly chopped	salt
5 slices bacon, grilled until crisp and roughly chopped	freshly ground black pepper
	1 tbsp double cream (optional)

Empty the tub of cheese into a medium-sized mixing bowl. Add all the other ingredients and mix together. Season to taste. If it is too sharp, add the cream. Put into a paté dish and chill for approximately 1–2 hours before serving.

Serve with toasted pitta bread.

John Leslie offers a new twist to mixing Parma ham with melon

Prue Leith's Grilled Mediterranean Vegetables

CHEF AND COOKERY WRITER

Serves 6

2 heads fennel	6 medium field mushrooms,
I large red pepper	tough stems removed
I large yellow pepper	extra virgin olive oil
2 small aubergines, sliced into 0.6 cm (¼ in)	*To garnish*
thick lengthwise strips	extra virgin olive oil
2 courgettes, sliced into 0.6 cm (¼ in) thick	sea salt
lengthwise strips	coarse freshly ground black pepper
6 spring onions, trimmed and sliced	fresh basil leaves
in half lengthwise if thick	squashy black olives

Heat the grill, grill pan, barbecue or oven grill to maximum. Slice the fennel into thick slices, leaving some stalk-end on each slice to hold the leaves together. Use a swivel peeler to remove the thin outer membrane of the peppers. Then cut them into sections down the creases and peel any edges previously missed. Cut each section in half. Place all the vegetables into a large bowl. Add the olive oil and turn all the vegetables in olive oil to coat.

Arrange the vegetables on the grill, grill pan, or on a foil-covered grill tray. Grill at the maximum heat to char both sides. Remove as they are done.

Serve warm or cold, drizzled with additional olive oil, seasoned generously with sea salt and freshly ground black pepper and garnished with sprigs of fresh basil and a few black olives.

Garlic Prawns

STEVE MOORE, WARWICKSHIRE

Serves 2

225 g (8 oz) large prawns,	I stick celery, thinly sliced
cooked and peeled	I apricot, thinly sliced (fresh or dried)
2 tbsp mayonnaise	225 g (8 oz) wild rice, cooked and cooled
2–3 cloves garlic, crushed	lemon to garnish

Combine all the ingredients in a mixing bowl. Serve chilled on a bed of wild rice. Garnish with a twist of lemon.

Spinach and Cream Cheese Parcels

MRS GERRY TANNER, SOMERSET

Serves 6

600 g (1 lb 6 oz) bought shortcrust pastry	100 g (4 oz) grated cheese
450 g (1 lb) cream cheese	2 tbsp tomato purée
225 g (½ lb) cooked spinach –	2 cloves garlic, crushed
or 450 g (1 lb) fresh spinach	½ tsp basil, freeze-dried
	½ tsp oregano, freeze-dried

Pre-heat the oven to 190°C/375°F/Gas 5. Place the cream cheese in a food processor and switch on at a low speed. Gradually add the remaining ingredients, increasing the speed all the time.

Cut the pastry into 9 cm (4 in) squares and place on a baking tray. Add two teaspoonfuls of the filling on each one and fold the pastry over to make triangles. Brush with beaten egg or milk, to glaze. Bake in the oven for 20 minutes or until firm to the touch.

Herring with Apples

INGEBORD VAN TEESELING, UTRECHT, NETHERLANDS

Serves 4

4 fresh herrings, cleaned and boned	150 ml (¼ pint) double cream
1 onion, thinly sliced	juice of ½ lemon
2½ tbsp caster sugar	100 g (4 oz) fromage frais
1 tsp dill	2 cooking apples, peeled and cored
½ tsp white pepper	2 extra tbsp lemon juice
1 tbsp cider vinegar	2 tsp fresh chives, chopped

Put the herrings to soak in cold water for 3 hours. Mix the sugar, dill, pepper and vinegar together. Stir in the onion. Dry the herrings with kitchen paper, and place them in the onion mixture. Cover and put in the fridge for 6 hours.

Beat the cream until it is not completely firm. Mix in the juice of half a lemon and fromage frais. Chop the apples and cook in the remaining lemon juice and a little water for 5–10 minutes. Mash them and lay on a plate. Add the herrings, and lay the cream mixture on top. Sprinkle with chives to garnish.

Raymond Blanc's Summer Tomato Tart Scented With Basil

CHEF AND COOKERY WRITER

Serves 4

250 g (9 oz) bought puff pastry, made with butter	salt
	8 very ripe tomatoes
For the topping	**For the garnish**
1 medium onion, finely chopped	4 tbsp olive oil, placed in a bowl
6 tbsp olive oil	8 black olives, stoned and quartered
leaves from 6 thyme sprigs	(optional)
freshly ground pepper	16 fresh basil leaves, shredded

This recipe comes from *Cooking for Friends* published by Hodder Headline.

Pre-heat the oven to 230°C/450°F/Gas 8 at least half an hour before baking. Place a lightly oiled pastry sheet on the lowest shelf for the last 15 minutes to get it really hot.

Preparing the puff pastry

Lightly flour the working surface. Cut the puff pastry into four, shape into balls, then roll out into rounds of about 18 cm (7 in) in diameter and 1–2 mm (1/16 in) thick. Place these rounds on a lightly floured tray and refrigerate for 5 minutes. Remove the rounds and trim to rounds of 16 cm (6½ in) in diameter. Brush another pastry sheet of approximately 40×35 cm (16×14 in) with a little olive oil and place the 4 pastry rounds on it. Refrigerate again.

With the remaining puff pastry prepare thin strips 1–2 mm (1/16 in) thick by 5 mm (¼ in) wide. Moisten the edges of the pastry circles with water, then curl the thin strips round the circles to make 'sides' for the tarts. Refrigerate.

Preparing the topping

Sweat the onion in the olive oil with the thyme leaves for about 8 minutes, add seasoning to taste, then cool and reserve.

Remove the eyes of the tomatoes, and halve them across the width. Remove the seeds leaving the flesh intact. Cut into rings approximately 3 mm (1/8 in) thick. Reserve.

Preparing and cooking the tomato tarts

Divide the onion between the pastry rounds, spreading it out over the base. Arrange tomato slices so that they overlap the onion. Brush the tomatoes and the edges of the pastry rounds with the olive oil from the bowl. Season.

Quickly remove the hot pastry sheet from the oven, and place the tarts on it, using a fish slice. Place on the lowest shelf in oven, and bake for 12 minutes.

Remove the tarts from the oven and sprinkle with the olives (if using) and shredded basil. Cook for a further 3 minutes, then remove from the oven. Cool for 5 minutes and serve.

Quick Smoked Fish Paté

LESLEY, KENT

Serves 6

225 g (8 oz) smoked mackerel or trout fillets, flaked	2 tsp dried dill
150 g (5 oz) natural yoghurt	I tbsp fresh chives, chopped
50 g (2 oz) margarine	I tsp horseradish sauce
2 tbsp lemon juice	salt
	freshly ground black pepper

For a textured paté, put all the ingredients in a bowl and mix well by hand. Place the mixture in a container and chill until required. For a smooth paté, mix using a hand blender or food processor. Serve with melba toast.

Potato Latkes (Pancakes)

NANCY GORE, BREAKTHROUGH FUNDRAISER

6 medium-sized potatoes, peeled and grated	50 g (2 oz) flour
I onion, skinned and finely chopped	pinch of salt
2 eggs, beaten	vegetable oil for frying

Mix the potatoes and onions and stir in the beaten eggs. Add the flour and salt. Heat the fat in a heavy frying pan. Divide the mixture into tablespoonfuls and fry until golden brown, turning once. Drain on kitchen paper, and serve piping hot.

Fiona Armstrong's Two-pear Starter

NEWSCASTER AND TV PRESENTER

Serves 2

1 avocado, peeled	1 tbsp vinaigrette
1 pear, peeled	assorted chopped fresh herbs

Slice the avocado and pear lengthways and arrange in a fan shape on a plate. Dress with the vinaigrette and herbs. Serve immediately, otherwise both pears may discolour.

Cliff Richard's Leek and Potato Soup

SINGER

Serves 4–6

50 g (2 oz) butter	1.2 litres (2 pints) chicken stock
450 g (1 lb) potatoes, peeled and cut into small chunks	mixed herbs, fresh or dried, to taste
	225 g (8 oz) leeks, chopped
2 onions, chopped	150 ml (5 fl oz) natural yoghurt

Melt the butter in a large pan and fry the potatoes and onions for a few minutes. Add the stock, herbs and leeks. Simmer until the potatoes are cooked. Allow to cool for 10 minutes. Mix in the yoghurt, then liquidize. Serve hot or cold.

Bill Wyman's Guacamole

MUSICIAN

Serves 4

2 ripe avocados	juice of ½ lemon
2 cloves garlic	½ tsp cayenne pepper
½ onion, chopped	pinch of white pepper
1 tomato, chopped	1 tsp Tabasco

This recipe comes from Bill's restaurant Sticky Fingers.

Roughly mash the avocados in a bowl. Crush the garlic and add to the bowl with the chopped onion, tomato, lemon juice, cayenne pepper, white pepper and Tabasco. Mix, but do not blend, the ingredients to create a chunky-textured dip.

Serve cold with Mexican corn chips.

Kevin Woodford's Casserole of Wild Mushrooms in a Meaux Mustard Sauce, Served on Toasted Muffins

CHEF AND COOKERY WRITER

Serves 1

100 g (4 oz) mixed wild mushrooms, sliced	1 tbsp French mustard
2 muffins	1 small glass Marsala wine
50 g (2 oz) butter	120 ml (4 fl oz) double cream
50 g (2 oz) onions, chopped	salt
1 garlic clove, crushed	2 tomatoes, skinned, seeded and chopped,
1 tbsp chervil, chopped	to garnish
a few black peppercorns, crushed	fresh basil leaves, to garnish

Pre-heat the oven to 180°C/350°F/Gas 4. Scoop out the centre of the muffins to make a bowl. Put to one side. Melt a little butter in a frying pan, add the onions, garlic, a little chervil and peppercorns. Then add the mushrooms, season and cook for a minute. Add the mustard, a little Marsala and the cream. Allow to simmer very gently for a few minutes. Check the seasoning.

Warm the muffins through in the oven, then remove them and fill with the mixture. Garnish with chopped tomatoes and basil leaves, and serve.

Toasted Avocado

MARY HOWSON, NOTTINGHAMSHIRE

Serves 4

2 avocados, peeled and thinly sliced	frisée lettuce
4 slices of granary bread	4 king prawns
25 g (1 oz) butter	1 lemon
225 g (8 oz) Blue Stilton cheese	

Toast the bread on one side and then thinly butter the other side. Divide the avocado into quarters, arrange on the buttered side of the bread and cover with thin slices of Stilton. Flash under a hot grill to melt the cheese and then serve immediately with a garnish of lettuce, king prawns and a lemon wedge.

Pakoras and Coconut Chutney

NANZEEN JAFFER

Serves 6-8

150 g (5 oz) plain flour	pinch of bicarbonate of soda
I onion, chopped	8 tbsp water
I potato, chopped into cubes	oil for deep frying
100 g (4 oz) frozen peas	*For the Chutney*
I tsp salt	½ cup desiccated coconut
¼ tsp ground black pepper	½ tsp salt
½ tsp ground cumin	3 or 4 fresh green chillies
small bunch of fresh coriander (optional)	juice of ½ a lemon

Heat oil gently. Meanwhile mix together all remaining *pakora* ingredients in a bowl, adding only enough water to make the mixture a dripping consistency.

Drop spoonfuls of the mixture into the moderately hot oil and fry for a few minutes, turning occasionally, until golden brown. Remove from the oil with a slotted spoon and place on a piece of kitchen paper to drain.

To make the chutney, place coconut, salt, green chillies and lemon juice in a blender and blend for several minutes. Serve with the warm *pakoras*.

Mediterranean Pasta Salad

DANIELLE PECK, LONDON

Serves 4-6

175 g (6 oz) pasta bows	3 tbsp olive oil
I small onion, chopped	2 tsp red pesto sauce (from a jar)
I clove garlic, crushed	½ tbsp tomato ketchup
2 courgettes, sliced	salt
I yellow pepper, chopped	freshly ground pepper
2 flat field mushrooms, sliced	

Cook pasta according to packet instructions. Heat 2 tbsp of the olive oil in a frying-pan and fry onion and garlic until golden. Add pepper and mushrooms to the pan and cook until soft. Add courgettes and fry for a further 2 minutes.

Mix in pesto and tomato ketchup and stir to coat vegetables and cook for 2 more minutes. Season to taste.

Drain pasta and return to saucepan then add vegetable mixture and remaining olive oil. Toss together and leave to cool. Serve on a bed of dark green salad leaves.

Moyra Fraser's Goats' Cheese and Roasted Pepper Salad

COOKERY EDITOR, GOOD HOUSEKEEPING

Serves 6

6 large peppers (preferably a mixture of red, green and yellow)	2 tbsp white wine vinegar or lemon juice
3-4 large garlic cloves	6 tbsp olive oil
1 level tsp Dijon mustard	12 thin slices of French bread
1 tsp runny honey	6 small rindless goats' cheeses, each weighing about 50 g (2 oz)
salt	mixed salad leaves
freshly ground black pepper	a few pine nuts, toasted
	a few chopped fresh herbs (optional)

Pre-heat the oven to180°C/350°F/Gas 4. Grill the whole peppers and garlic cloves (still in their skins) under a very hot grill for 10–15 minutes or until soft and blackened all over, turning occasionally.

Remove the skin from the garlic and squeeze the soft insides into a jug. Add the mustard, honey and plenty of salt and pepper. Beat together with a fork, mashing the garlic as you beat. Gradually beat in the vinegar or lemon juice followed by the oil. Taste and add more salt and pepper if necessary. Carefully peel the blackened skin from the peppers, halve them and remove the cores and seeds. Cut the flesh into strips and place in a shallow dish. Pour the dressing over the peppers.

Just before serving, toast the bread slices on both sides. Halve the cheeses and place one half on each slice of toast. Arrange on a baking tray and bake in the oven for 8 to 12 minutes or until the cheese is soft and warmed through, but not completely melted.

Meanwhile, arrange the salad leaves on six plates, and spoon over the peppers and marinade. Arrange the bread slices and baked cheeses on top and sprinkle with a few toasted pine nuts and fresh herbs, if using. Season with black pepper and serve immediately.

Siân Lloyd's Spicy Bean Salad

WEATHER FORECASTER

Serves 6–8

2×425 g (15 oz) tins red kidney beans, rinsed and drained	2 tbsp capers, chopped
	1 tbsp fresh basil, chopped
1 green pepper, seeded and chopped	4 tbsp chopped fresh parsley
1 dill pickle, diced	1 tbsp fresh tarragon, chopped
For the dressing	2 tsp chilli powder
120 ml (4 fl oz) olive oil	a few drops Tabasco
120 ml (4 fl oz) red wine vinegar	1 tsp sugar
4 tbsp chopped spring onions	½ tsp sea salt, to taste
1–2 garlic cloves, chopped	freshly ground black pepper, to taste

Mix the beans, pepper and dill pickle together in a bowl and place in the fridge to chill.

Just before serving, combine the oil, vinegar, parsley, spring onions, garlic, capers and herbs with the chilli powder, Tabasco and sugar. Mix well and add the salt and pepper to taste. Pour the dressing over the bean salad and toss.

Serve with pieces of fresh French baguette to mop up the dressing.

Salad with Walnut Oil Dressing and Roquefort

ANGELA RYAN, KENT

Serves 4

mixed salad leaves	6 tbsp walnut oil
175 g (6 oz) Roquefort cheese, diced	seasoning
For the dressing	50 g (2 oz) walnuts
3 tbsp cider vinegar	crusty bread
2 tsp Dijon mustard	

Divide the salad leaves evenly between four plates then sprinkle the cheese on top. Just prior to serving, mix the cider vinegar, Dijon mustard, walnut oil and seasoning to make the dressing and pour over the salad leaves. Scatter the walnut pieces on top and serve with crusty bread.

Watercress Soup

KAY DOBER, SOUTH GLAMORGAN

Serves 4

2 medium-sized potatoes, diced	2 bunches watercress, de-stalked and
1 medium-sized onion, diced	chopped (a few sprigs reserved for garnish)
1 clove garlic	salt
50 g (2 oz) butter	freshly ground black pepper
900 ml (1½ pints) vegetable stock	1 small carton natural yoghurt

Soften the potatoes, onion and garlic in the butter in a large saucepan. Add the stock and bring to the boil. Add the watercress, bring back to the boil, then turn down the heat and simmer for 20 minutes. Season to taste. Remove from heat, allow to cool, and then liquidize. Reheat and serve, garnished with sprigs of watercress and a swirl of natural yoghurt.

Fresh and Peppery Seafood Starter

LORELY MASKELL, KENT

Serves 4

200 g (7 oz) watercress	6–8 tbsp mayonnaise
2 ripe avocados	½ tsp paprika
lemon juice	½ tsp turmeric
1 medium pink grapefruit (or orange)	4 sprigs of parsley, to serve
100 g (4 oz) peeled prawns	

Wash the watercress and arrange in a large shallow dish to form a bed. Halve the avocados, remove the stone then cut off the skin. Cut into slices (not too fine) and sprinkle with lemon juice to prevent browning. Peel the grapefruit and skin the segments. Conserve as much of the juice as possible. Arrange alternating slices of avocado and grapefruit on the bed of watercress, pour over the grapefruit juice and tumble the prawns into the centre. Mix the paprika and turmeric with the mayonnaise and spoon over the prawns. Decorate with the sprigs of parsley and serve.

Mediterranean Rice Salad

MRS PALMER, EAST SUSSEX

Serves 4–6

225 g (8 oz) of Italian rice	6 tomatoes, chopped
4 tbsp olives, halved	1 tsp pine kernels
⅓ cucumber, chopped	50 g (2 oz) Parmesan, to serve
1 yellow pepper, chopped	50 g (2 oz) sultanas

Cook the rice according to packet instructions. Stir-fry the olives, cucumber, pepper and tomatoes for about two minutes. Add the pine kernels and sultanas. Pour olive oil over the mixture to coat it, and add grated Parmesan before you serve.

Slimmer Clubs UK Melon Soup

MARGARET TURNER, OXON

Serves 3

1 Galia melon	juice of 2 lemons
3 tbsp spring onions, chopped	300 ml (½ pint) vegetable stock
1 tsp root ginger, finely chopped	3 slices lemon and mint leaves to garnish

Halve the melon and discard seeds. Scoop out the flesh and put into saucepan. Add spring onions, ginger, lemon juice and vegetable stock, cover and simmer for 15 minutes.

Add contents of saucepan to blender and process until smooth.

Return to saucepan and reheat before serving, or serve chilled. Garnish with lemon slices and mint leaves.

Spiced Parsnips

JENNY BURRELL, LEICESTERSHIRE

Serves 4

1 kg (2¼ lb) parsnips, quartered	1 tbsp grainy mustard
25 g (1 oz) butter	seasoning

Par-boil parsnips for about 6 minutes. Melt the butter in a frying pan, and add the mustard and seasoning, drain the parsnips and transfer into frying pan. Cook gently, turning the parsnips occasionally to ensure they are well-coated. Cook until tender.

Radicchio and Goats' Cheese Parcels

DANIELLE NAY, LONDON

Serves 4

4-1cm (½-inch) thick slices of goats' cheese, chilled	8 large basil leaves
4 large radicchio leaves	4 large sundried tomatoes
25 g (1 oz) pine kernels	8 tbsp olive oil
	black pepper

Wrap each slice of cheese in a radicchio leaf. Place each 'parcel' seam–side down on a baking tray and brush with oil. Scatter with the pine nuts and press them gently down. Grill under a very hot grill for 1-2 minutes until the pine nuts turn brown. Serve decorated with shredded basil leaves and sundried tomatoes.

Cleo Rocos' Adonis Eggs

TV PERSONALITY

Serves 2

15 g (½ oz) butter	2 eggs
1 tomato, chopped	salt and pepper
65 g (2½ oz) feta cheese	2 slices bread

Melt the butter in a frying pan. Add the chopped tomato and the feta cheese and stir until it melts. Break the eggs on the top of the mixture and poach them. When the cheese is really gooey and the eggs are set, add salt and pepper to taste. Serve hot on the slices of bread.

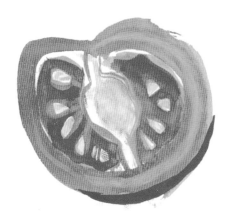

MAIN COURSES

Jane Horrocks' Honey Chicken with Grapes and Almonds

ACTRESS

Serves 2

2 chicken pieces	salt and freshly ground pepper
I tbsp clear honey	a few blanched almonds
I tbsp peanut oil	a few green grapes
I tbsp dry or medium sherry	25 g (I oz) butter
½ tbsp light soy sauce	

re-heat the oven to 180°C/350°F/Gas 4. Place the chicken pieces in a casserole dish.
Mix the honey, oil, sherry, soy sauce, salt and pepper together and brush the chicken with some of the mixture. Cook for 40–50 minutes brushing on the remaining mixture at intervals during the cooking. Immediately prior to serving, gently fry the almonds and grapes in the butter for a few minutes, then scatter over the chicken pieces.
Serve with new potatoes and courgettes.

Cod with Cucumber Sauce

PAULINE WHITING, BERKSHIRE

Serves 4

4 cod fillets	*For the cucumber sauce*
25 g (I oz) butter	½ cucumber
I orange	100 g (4 oz) plain yoghurt
	seasoning

Pre-heat the oven to 180°C/350°F/Gas 4. Place the pieces of fish in a well-buttered baking dish just large enough to accommodate them. Using a potato peeler, pare strips of rind from the orange, then squeeze out the juice. Pour the juice over the fish, add the rind, and season to taste. Cover with foil and bake for 20 minutes.

While the fish is cooking, make the cucumber sauce. Cut a few slices of cucumber and reserve for garnishing, then dice the rest. Mix the diced cucumber and yoghurt together, and season.

When the fish is cooked, remove the orange peel, pour the cucumber sauce over the fish, garnish with a few cucumber slices and serve.

Italian Cottage Cheese

SUSAN KEMP, WEST YORKSHIRE

Serves 4

I large onion, chopped	½ tsp dried basil
I large clove of garlic, crushed	½ tsp dried oregano
2 tbsp olive oil	250g (9oz) natural cottage cheese
450 g (I lb) courgettes, sliced	freshly ground black pepper
400 g (14 oz) tin chopped tomatoes	salt

Gently fry the onions and garlic in the olive oil until they are transparent. Add the courgettes and cook for a further 10 minutes or until soft. Stir in the tomatoes, herbs, salt and pepper and continue to cook for 5 minutes. Stir the mixture well, then cover with the cottage cheese. Increase the heat to ensure that the cheese is cooked and serve with pasta.

Toby Anstis' Spaghetti Bolognese

TV PRESENTER

Serves 4

1 tbsp sunflower oil	400 g (14 oz) tin chopped tomatoes with
450 g (1 lb) best minced beef	garlic or basil
1 onion, chopped	half a glass of red wine
1 green pepper, chopped	salt
2 cloves, crushed	freshly ground black pepper
8 mushrooms, chopped	250 g (9 oz) spaghetti
2 tbsp tomato purée	grated Parmesan, to garnish

Put the oil in a large frying pan and add the mince in small batches. Stir until all the meat is completely browned. Add the onion, pepper and garlic. Stir and cook for a further 5 minutes over a fairly low heat. Add the mushrooms, tomato purée, tin of tomatoes and the red wine. Season well. Simmer for another 15–20 minutes.

Meanwhile, cook the pasta according to the packet instructions. Drain. Add the pasta

Wendy Craig's Spicy Chicken Drumsticks

ACTRESS

Serves 6

6 chicken drumsticks	1 tsp dark brown sugar
4 tbsp wine vinegar	3 tbsp Worcestershire sauce
1 tsp made mustard	4 tbsp olive oil

Using a knife, deeply slash the skin of the drumsticks in several places. Mix the rest of the ingredients together in a shallow dish. Coat the drumsticks, or better still marinate for a few hours, turning from time to time.

Heat the grill or barbecue. When hot grill the drumsticks for about 25 minutes, turning frequently until the meat is cooked (pierce the flesh to make sure the juices run clear) and the skin is crisp.

Serve with rice salad.

Wendy Craig hots up the Challenge with her Spicy Chicken Drumsticks

Josie Lawrence's Quick Vegetable Pasta Sauce

COMEDIENNE

Serves 2

225 g (8 oz) mushrooms, diced	1 tbsp pesto sauce (from a jar)
225 g (8 oz) courgettes, diced	1 tbsp low-fat fromage frais
2 cloves garlic, crushed	oregano
25 g (1 oz) low-fat margarine	basil
200 g (7 oz) tin chopped tomatoes	

Fry the mushroom, courgettes and garlic in the low-fat margarine until soft. Drain off the margarine. In a second pan mix together the tomatoes and pesto sauce. Add the cooked vegetables and place the pan on a low heat. When it is warmed through, remove the pan from the heat and stir in the fromage frais until the sauce is thick and creamy. Sprinkle the oregano and basil over the sauce and stir. Mix the sauce with your chosen cooked pasta.

Will Carling's Chicken Parcels

ENGLAND RUGBY UNION CAPTAIN

Serves 6

6 chicken breasts, with the skins removed	1 tsp freshly ground black pepper
4 cloves garlic, chopped	4 tbsp orange juice
1½ tsp salt	4 tbsp lemon juice
1 tsp chopped oregano	olive oil
1 tsp ground cumin	

Dry the chicken pieces with a paper towel and place in a large bowl. Combine the garlic, salt, oregano, cumin, pepper and fruit juices. Pour over the chicken, cover and leave to marinate for 24 hours in the fridge, turning two or three times.

Pre-heat the oven to 180°C/350°F/Gas 4. If you have individual clay pots use these or, alternatively, cut kitchen foil into six 30 cm (12 in) squares and brush each side with oil. Divide the chicken pieces among the squares and spoon the marinade equally over each, holding the edges up to avoid spilling. Fold the foil over the chicken and seal the edges tightly.

Arrange the foil envelopes in a baking dish and bake for 1½ hours or until the chicken is tender and the juices run clear. Open a parcel carefully and check after one hour.

When cooked slit open the envelopes and serve with hot tortillas or crusty bread to mop up the juices.

Spinach, Mushroom and Almond Ring

MRS ADÈLE FULLER, BERKSHIRE

Serves 6

2 tbsp olive oil	2 tbsp double cream
I onion, chopped	200 g (7 oz) packet frozen spinach
I clove garlic, crushed	½ tsp dried tarragon
I kg (2 lb) mixed mushrooms, chopped	400 g (14 oz) box filo pastry
I tsp soy sauce	I egg yolk, mixed with a little milk
salt	2 oz flaked almonds
ground black pepper	

This recipe has been adapted by Sarah Brown, the vegetarian cookery writer.
Pre-heat the oven to 200°C/400°F/Gas 6. Heat the oil and gently cook the onion and garlic. Add the mushrooms. Cook until soft and season with soy sauce, salt and pepper to taste. Mix in the cream. Remove mixture from pan with slotted spoon, and set aside. (The pan juices can be thickened with a little cornflour to make a sauce to serve later with the ring.) Cook the spinach according to the packet instructions. Drain well, mix in the tarragon and season well.

Place overlapping pieces of the filo pastry onto a baking sheet in a circle, reserving about 4 rectangles for later. Brush well with the egg mixture. Place the spinach over the pastry, leaving enough of an edge to fold over later.

Top this with the mushroom mixture. Sprinkle over the flaked almonds. Fold up the edges of the pastry ring and then cover with the reserved filo pastry pieces, laying them over the ring diagonally and tucking the edges carefully underneath. Brush with remaining egg mixture.

Bake for 20 minutes until crisp and golden. Remove and slide from the baking tray onto a serving dish. Serve with new potatoes or wild rice and the vegetable of your choice.

Chicken in Marsala Wine with Orange and Shallots

AMY WILLCOCK, SOUTH GLAMORGAN

Serves 4–6

2 tbsp plain flour	16 shallots, peeled and left whole
salt	6 garlic cloves, peeled and left whole
freshly ground black pepper	300 ml (10 fl oz) Marsala
1 heaped tsp ground cardamom	300 ml (10 fl oz) orange juice, freshly
½ tsp ground coriander	squeezed
8 pieces of chicken (either a jointed chicken	1 tbsp Sherry vinegar
or breasts cut in half)	1 cinnamon stick
2 tbsp olive oil	1 tbsp crème fraiche
3 rashers bacon	

Season the flour with salt, pepper, cardamom, coriander and mix well. Coat each piece of chicken with the flour mixture and set aside. In a shallow ovenproof casserole dish heat the olive oil and cook the bacon, chicken, shallots and garlic until all are caramelized and a nutty brown colour. Next add the Marsala, orange juice, Sherry vinegar and cinnamon. Stir and simmer on top of the hotplate for approximately 40 minutes, until the juices from the chicken pieces run clear. When cooked, stir in the crème fraiche and serve with brown rice and a green salad.

Sliced Potatoes and Leeks

CLARE FORRESTER, BREAKTHROUGH FUNDRAISER

Serves 2

25 g (1 oz) butter	salt
2 medium-sized leeks	freshly ground pepper
4 large potatoes	

Pre-heat the oven to 220°C/425°F/Gas 7.
Grease a casserole or large mixing bowl with the butter. Wash the leeks thoroughly, trim and slice. Peel the potatoes, and slice very finely. Put the potatoes and leeks in the dish in layers, finishing with potatoes.

Season and cook in the oven for at least an hour.

Stuffed Trout

KATH BARBER, SOUTH YORKSHIRE

Serves 4

4 rainbow trout, gutted and boned	**25 g (1 oz) walnuts, finely chopped**
For the Stuffing	**50–75 g (2–3 oz) chopped prunes**
25 g (1 oz) butter	**2 tsp fresh parsley, chopped**
½ onion, finely chopped	**50 g (2 oz) fresh white breadcrumbs**
1 small clove garlic, crushed	**½ egg, beaten**

Pre-heat the oven to 190°C/375°F/Gas 5.

In a frying pan melt the butter, and fry onion and garlic until soft. Add the remaining ingredients, except the egg, and stir. When well mixed add the egg to bind.

Place the prepared fish in pieces of well-buttered foil, and fill with the stuffing. Leave parcels open and bake for 20-30 minutes.

Spaghetti Gallese

BRONWEN EVANS, BUCKINGHAMSHIRE

Serves 4–6

4 leeks	**1 carton of passata sieved tomatoes**
generous glass of white wine	**400 g (14 oz) spaghetti**
1 clove garlic, crushed	**3–4 tbsp Italian cream cheese,**
pinch of basil	**e.g. mascarpone**
pinch of oregano	**Parmesan, to serve**

Finely chop the leeks and simmer in wine, garlic and herbs until the leeks are soft. Add passata and cook for 15 minutes. Simmer, stirring occasionally, until sauce has thickened.

Meanwhile, cook spaghetti according to packet instructions. When spaghetti is cooked remove sauce from heat and stir in the cheese. Drain the spaghetti and add to sauce.

Phillip Schofield's Potato Scones

TV PERSONALITY

Serves 4–6

750 g (1½ lb) potatoes, peeled and freshly boiled	**50 g (2 oz) butter**
	salt and freshly ground black pepper
150 ml (5 fl oz) milk	**50 g (2 oz) self-raising flour**

Pre-heat the oven to 180°C/350°F/Gas 4. Mash the potatoes and gradually add the milk and butter. Add the salt and pepper to taste. Mix in enough flour to form a stiff dough. On a floured board, roll out the dough and, using a saucer as a guide, cut into individual circles measuring 13 cm (5 in) wide and 1 cm (½ in) thick. Place on the top shelf of oven and cook for 15–20 minutes until golden brown. Serve immediately.

Cheryl Baker's Blue Cheese Pie

TV PERSONALITY

Serves 4

50 g (2 oz) blue cheese, crumbled	**225 g (8 oz) puff pastry**
150 ml (5 fl oz) double cream	**1 egg, beaten**
2 eggs, beaten	**salt**
a sprinkling of raisins soaked in brandy	

Pre-heat the oven to 220°C/425°F/Gas 7.

Roll out the pastry thinly and line a 20 cm (8 in) flan tin. Leave enough pastry to roll out a 20 cm (8 in) circle for the top.

Mix the cheese, cream and the 2 beaten eggs together. Stir in the raisins. Pour the mixture into the pastry shell and top with the pastry circle. Seal the edges. Brush with the other beaten egg and sprinkle salt on top.

Bake for 20–25 minutes until risen and golden.

Cheryl Baker just keeps rolling along

Duck with Sage in Red Wine

DEREK KEWLEY, EAST SUSSEX

Serves 4

3 onions, sliced into rings	2 tbsp plain flour
75 g (3 oz) smoked gammon ham, chopped into fat matchsticks	600 ml (1 pint) red wine
75 g (3 oz) salted butter	12 sage leaves, chopped
4 medium duck breasts	1 sprig each of fresh oregano, rosemary and parsley
salt	12 small wild mushrooms
freshly ground black pepper	

Pre-heat the oven to 180°C/350°F/Gas 4.

Fry the onions and ham in the butter until the onions are golden. Remove from the frying pan retaining as much butter in the pan as possible. Place the onions and ham in a casserole dish.

Prick the duck breasts all over with a fork, season both sides with salt, pepper and coat with the flour. Fry in the retained butter until golden and add to the casserole dish. Add the red wine, herbs and wild mushrooms. Season to taste. Put in the oven and cook for 1¼ hours.

Pork and Apricot Casserole

SHEENAGH SLATER, BERWICKSHIRE

Serves 4–6

2 onions, finely chopped	225 g (8 oz) dried apricots
50 g (2 oz) butter	50 g (2 oz) raisins
1 kg (2 lb) lean pork, cubed	450 ml (15 fl oz) chicken stock
salt	juice of ½ lemon
freshly ground black pepper	1–2 tbsp apricot jam
½ tsp cinnamon	

Sauté the onions in the butter. Brown the meat, season lightly and add cinnamon. Stir in the apricots and raisins and sauté a little longer. Add stock and bring slowly to the boil. Simmer gently for 1½–2 hours. Flavour to taste with lemon juice and apricot jam and simmer for a further 15 minutes before serving.

John Barnes' Stir-fry Spicy Chicken and Rice

FOOTBALLER

Serves 4–6

75 g (3 oz) rice per person	1 green pepper, seeded
2 tbsp sunflower oil	1 red pepper, seeded
4 chicken breasts, cut into thin strips	225 g (8 oz) mushrooms
1 onion, chopped	1 jar spicy chicken sauce
2 courgettes	

Cook the rice according to the packet instructions. Heat 1 tablespoon of the oil in a large frying pan and add the chicken strips. Cook, stirring, for 10 minutes.

Chop the onion, courgettes, peppers and mushrooms into bite-sized pieces. Heat the other tablespoon of oil in a large wok, and fry the onion for 2 minutes. Then add the other chopped vegetables. Cook for a further 5 minutes. Add the chicken strips to the wok and pour over the jar of sauce. Cover the wok and simmer for 10 minutes. Serve hot with boiled rice.

Vanessa Binns' Bacon-wrapped Potato Cake

MASTERCHEF WINNER

Serves 4

1 kg (2 lb) baking potatoes, peeled and thinly sliced	225 g (8 oz) streaky bacon, rinded
knob of butter	75 g (3 oz) Gruyère cheese, grated
	freshly ground black pepper

Pre-heat the oven to 180°C/350°F/Gas 4. Simmer the sliced potatoes in lightly salted water for 5 minutes. Drain and reserve. Meanwhile, butter a 23cm (9in) quiche dish and line with the bacon allowing the rashers to overhang the edges of the dish. Put one-third of the potatoes in an even layer in the bottom of the dish, sprinkle with a third of the cheese and season with black pepper. Repeat this process twice. Fold back the overhanging bacon to cover the potatoes.

Bake in the oven for approximately 45 minutes until the potatoes are cooked and the bacon is crispy. Turn out onto a dish and grill the bottom to crisp the bacon. Cut into wedges and serve immediately.

Chilli Con Carne

STEPHANIE ROSE, SOMERSET

Serves 4

1 tbsp oil	1 green pepper, seeded and cubed
1 large onion, chopped	1 tbsp tomato purée
450 g (1 lb) minced beef	400 g (14 oz) tin tomatoes
1 tsp salt	425 g (15 oz) tin red kidney beans
3 tsp chilli powder	

Heat the oil in a large pan and fry the onion until soft. Add the mince in batches and stir over a medium heat until brown. Add the salt and chilli powder to taste and mix well. Stir in the green pepper, tomato purée and tomatoes and simmer for 20 minutes. Add the kidney beans and cook, stirring occasionally, for a further 20 minutes.

Serve with boiled rice and a green salad.

Suzanne Dando's Pork Escalopes with Calvados and Cream

GYMNAST AND TV PRESENTER

Serves 4

25 g (1 oz) butter	50 g (2 oz) oyster mushrooms
1 tbsp olive oil	2 tsp fresh sage, finely chopped
4 pork escalopes	3 tbsp double cream
1 onion, thinly sliced	salt
450 ml (15 fl oz) chicken or vegetable stock	freshly ground black pepper
2 tbsp Calvados (more if preferred)	1 apple, unpeeled, cored and sliced into rings

Heat the butter and olive oil in a large frying pan and brown the escalopes quickly on both sides. Remove the escalopes and gently fry the onions in the remaining fat until they have softened. Return the escalopes to the pan, add the stock and simmer for 15–20 minutes. Then add the Calvados, mushrooms and sage, and season. Simmer for a further 5 minutes before removing the pan from the heat and stirring in the cream. Garnish with the apple rings and serve with a green salad.

Michael Van Straten's
Courgette Pasta

RADIO PERSONALITY

Serves I

I tbsp vegetable oil	25 g (I oz) butter
I tbsp salt	I tbsp freshly grated Parmesan cheese
100 g (3½ oz) spaghettini	freshly ground black pepper
I small courgette	

This recipe comes from Michael's book *Superfast Foods*.
Bring a large pan of water to the boil and add the oil, salt and pasta. Grate the courgette using a fine grater. When the pasta is cooked according to the packet instructions, drain and immediately transfer to a hot dish, add the courgette, butter, Parmesan and seasoning. Toss and eat immediately.

Julie Goodyear's
Corned Beef Hash

ACTRESS

Serves I

I medium onion, chopped	dash of hot pepper sauce e.g. Tabasco
100 g (4 oz) corned beef, chopped	½ beef stock cube, crumbled
¼ tsp dried basil, or 2 leaves	75 g (3 oz) potatoes, cooked and sliced
fresh basil, chopped	2 tsp margarine

Pre-heat the oven to 190°C/375°F/Gas 5. Place the onion in a pan of boiling water and cook for 3–4 minutes. Drain and reserve the cooking liquid.
Mix together the corned beef, onion, basil and pepper sauce, and spoon into a small ovenproof dish. Dissolve the stock cube in 5 tablespoons of the reserved liquid, and pour over the corned beef mixture. Top with the sliced potatoes and dot with the margarine. Bake in the oven for 20–30 minutes until the potato is beginning to brown.

Coca-Cola Chicken

MRS LEE, TAYSIDE

Serves 2

2 chicken breasts	**2 tbsp tomato ketchup**
I can Coca-Cola	

Pre-heat the oven to 190°C/375°F/Gas 5. Place the chicken in a deep baking dish. Pour over the Coca-Cola and the ketchup and bake in the oven for 1–1½ hours.

Sankha Guha's Skate in Black Butter

TV PERSONALITY

Serves 6

1.5 kg (3 lb) skate (middle pieces of the wing are best)	**2 tbsp white wine vinegar**
1.2 litres (2 pints) fish stock	**3 tbsp capers**
100 g (4 oz) butter	**2 tbsp parsley finely chopped**

Put the skate pieces in the boiling stock, lower the heat and simmer for 15 minutes. Drain the skate pieces (discarding the cooking liquid) and put them in a warmed dish.

To make the black butter, melt the butter in a frying pan and cook until it foams golden brown, then pour it over the skate. Put the vinegar into the pan and bubble for a few seconds before pouring over the fish too. Finally, scatter with capers and parsley and serve.

Prawn Salad

POTATO MARKETING BOARD

Serves 4

450 g (I lb) new potatoes, cooked and halved	**2 tbsp sesame seeds**
120 g (4½ oz) mushrooms, thinly sliced	***For the dressing***
I red pepper, seeded and sliced into strips	**3 tbsp soy sauce**
I green pepper, seeded and sliced into strips	**I tbsp lemon juice**
	I tsp brown sugar
225 g (8 oz) cooked prawns, peeled	**2 tbsp vegetable oil**

Mix all the raw vegetables together with the potatoes, prawns and place in a serving dish. Mix the soy sauce, lemon juice, sugar and oil in a container with lid and shake well. Just before serving, pour the salad dressing over the vegetables.

Kirsty McCaskill's Veggie Chilli

WEATHER FORECASTER'S DAUGHTER

Serves 2

I tbsp oil	425 g (15 oz) can red kidney
I onion, chopped	beans, drained
I garlic clove, crushed	I tsp dried oregano or marjoram
I red, green or yellow pepper,	I tsp chilli powder
cored, seeded and chopped	salt
I–2 tomatoes, finely chopped	freshly ground black pepper

This recipe is taken from the *Oxfam Vegetarian Cookbook*.

Heat the oil in a large saucepan, add the onion and cook until softened, then add the garlic and cook gently for 1 minute. Add the remaining ingredients, stir well, cover and cook for 20 minutes.

Serve with rice or brown bread.

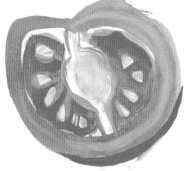

Potato and Leek Meat Loaf

CLARE FORRESTER, BREAKTHROUGH FUNDRAISER

Serves 4

450 g (1 lb) minced beef	I egg, beaten
I packet potato and leek dried soup mix	2 tbsp water
2 tsp dried rosemary	

Pre-heat the oven to 180°C/350°F/Gas 4 and grease a 450 g (1 lb) loaf tin.

Mix the minced beef, dried soup and the rosemary together. Add the egg, and as much of the water as necessary to bind. Press the mixture gently into the tin and cook in the oven for about 1¼ hours. Remove and cool a little before cutting into slices to serve. This is also very good served cold.

Anna Walker's Cannes Chicken

TV PRESENTER

Serves 4

1 iceberg lettuce, shredded	4 chicken breasts, chopped into
1 bunch watercress, trimmed	bite-sized pieces
2 mangoes, sliced	4 tsp soy sauce
sesame oil	4 tsp honey

Arrange the lettuce, watercress and mangoes on four plates. Fry the chicken breasts in the sesame oil. Add the soy sauce and honey and continue frying until golden brown. Arrange the chicken on top of the salad.

Lamburgers

MARGO McDONALD, SURREY

Makes 8 burgers

1 lb minced lamb	1 tbsp tomato purée
2 oz brown breadcrumbs	1 clove garlic
1 medium onion, very finely chopped	1 egg
2 tsp mint sauce	freshly ground black pepper

Place all ingredients in a food mixer and mix for a good 5 minutes, remove from the mixing bowl and shape into 8 good-sized burgers, and grill.

Delicious in summer cooked on a barbecue and served with a green salad and new potatoes, or in winter grilled and served with baked potatoes and lots of fresh vegetables.

Linda Lusardi's Pasta with Tuna

ACTRESS/TV PRESENTER

Serves 1

100 g (4 oz) pasta shells	low-fat salad cream
200 g (7 oz) tin of tuna in brine, drained	salt
200 g (7 oz) tin of sweetcorn, drained	pepper
1 tomato, chopped	vinegar, to taste

Bring a large pan of water to the boil, add pasta and cook according to the packet instructions.

Drain pasta and return to pan, add the tuna, sweetcorn, tomato, salad cream, salt, pepper and vinegar to taste. Stir over a low heat to warm through.

Serve warm with a crisp green salad.

Anna Walker takes us to the south of France with her Cannes Chicken

Veggie Burgers

HELEN HENDRY, FIFE

Serves 4

175 g (6 oz) fresh wholemeal breadcrumbs	1 size 1 egg
100 g (4 oz) button mushrooms, finely chopped	½ tsp celery salt
	½ tsp garlic salt
100 g (4 oz) onion, chopped	olive oil for frying
100 g (4 oz) cashew nuts, ground	

Reserve about half of the breadcrumbs on a plate for coating the burgers. Place all the ingredients in a bowl and mix well. Roll the mixture into 8 balls, flatten them and roll in the reserved crumbs to coat. Fry or grill them for about 4 minutes on each side.

Mediterranean Cheese Pasties

NOGA ZIVAN, LEICESTERSHIRE

Makes 10

350 g (12 oz) puff pastry	salt
250 g (9 oz) fromage frais	freshly ground pepper
250 g (9 oz) cottage cheese	sesame seeds
1 egg, separated	

Pre-heat the oven to 200°C/400°F/Gas 6. Roll out puff pastry to about 2 mm (1/16 in) thick and cut into 10 cm (4 in) squares. Mix together fromage frais, cottage cheese, egg yolk, salt and pepper. Place some of the cheese mixture in the middle of each pastry square. Fold the square over to form a triangle and seal the edges. Brush with beaten egg white and sprinkle the sesame seeds over the pastry. Bake in oven for about 20 minutes, until risen and slightly brown. They are best served freshly baked.

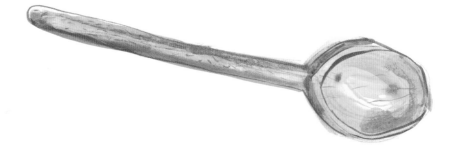

Bruce Roberts' Brewster's Pie

ACTOR

Serves 4–6

4 tbsp plain flour	225 g (8 oz) bacon rashers, roughly chopped
I tsp salt	50 g (2 oz) onion, chopped
freshly ground black pepper	50 g (2 fl oz) red wine (optional)
450 g (I lb) boned chicken	350 g (12 oz) puff pastry
I tbsp vegetable oil	I egg yolk, lightly beaten

Pre-heat the oven to 220°C/425°F/Gas 7 and butter a 20 cm (8 in) pie dish.
Mix the flour with the salt and pepper. Slice the chicken into small pieces and then coat with the seasoned flour. Heat the oil in a heavy based frying pan and brown the bacon and the onion. Remove it from the frying pan with a slotted spoon and set aside. Add the chicken and wine (if using) to the pan and cook over a gentle heat for 10–15 minutes. Then stir in the browned bacon and onion.

Cut the block of pastry roughly in half. Roll out the first half on a floured board and line the pie dish. Now add the filling. Roll out the other half of the pastry to fit over the top of the pie. Moisten the edges of the pastry with water and place the lid on top of the pie. Pinch lightly all the way round to seal. Brush the top of the pie with the egg yolk.

Bake in the oven for 20 minutes or until the pastry is lightly browned. Serve with a side salad.

Fisherman's Crumble

RICHARD TURLEY, WEST SUSSEX

Serves 4

2 tbsp lemon juice	¾ pint milk
2 tbsp vegetable oil	I tbsp chopped parsley
225 g (8 oz) smoked fish	2 tbsp cornflour
225 g (8 oz) white fish	75 g (3 oz) fresh breadcrumbs
4 spring onions, chopped	75 g (3 oz) grated cheese

Pre-heat the oven to 180°C/350°F/Gas 4.
Heat the lemon juice and the oil in a frying pan. Add the flaked fish and chopped spring onions. Cook over a low heat for 10 minutes. Warm the milk in a small saucepan. Add the butter and whisking continuously, sprinkle in the cornflour. Stir until the sauce has thickened slightly then add the parsley. Pour over the fish and mix together. Put in an ovenproof dish and top with the breadcrumbs and grated cheese.

Cook in the oven for about 20 minutes until golden brown.

Chicken and Peppers in Cider Sauce

BRYN GILMORE, SHROPSHIRE

Serves 4–6

2 tbsp plain white flour	2 peppers (preferably different colours)
pinch of salt	seeded and cut into strips
ground black pepper	300 ml (½ pint) strong dry cider
1 ¾ lb chicken, jointed and skinned	1 tsp dried thyme
2 tbsp olive oil	1 tsp dried basil
1 onion, peeled and chopped	100 g (4 oz) mushrooms, sliced

Mix flour with salt and pepper and coat the chicken pieces. Reserve the remaining flour. Heat 1 tbsp of the oil in the bottom of a large non-stick casserole. Add the chicken pieces and brown on all sides. Remove from pan.

Add the remaining oil to the pan and add the onion and peppers. Cook until onion is softened but not brown. Add the remaining seasoned flour, and stir carefully over medium heat for 1–2 minutes. Slowly add the cider, stirring constantly, to form a creamy sauce.

Return the chicken pieces to the pan and add the thyme and basil. Cover and simmer for approx. 45 minutes until the chicken is very tender and the juices run clear when pierced with a knife. A little water or cider may be added during cooking if required. Add the sliced mushrooms approx. 10 minutes before the end of the cooking time.

Serve hot with either new potatoes or crusty French bread, accompanied by a chilled glass of cider.

Mushrooms Nero

KEITH WARWICK, BEDFORDSHIRE

Serves 4

1 kg (2¼ lb) large flat mushrooms	salt
175 g (6 oz) butter	freshly ground pepper
2 cloves garlic, crushed	375 g (13 oz) egg noodles
2 glasses red wine	

Wipe the mushrooms with kitchen paper and slice thinly. Melt the butter in a large frying pan with a lid, and add the garlic and mushrooms. Gently cook the mushrooms with the lid on for 15 minutes. Add the wine and seasoning, stir and continue cooking without the lid. Cook until the liquid has been reduced and it resembles a black buttery liqueur.

While the mushrooms are cooking, boil the egg noodles in fast boiling water according to the instructions on the packet. Serve the mushrooms immediately on a bed of noodles.

Ken Hom's Thai Pasta with Champagne

CHEF AND COOKERY WRITER

Serves 8

500 g (just over 1 lb) egg noodles	glass of champagne
3 tbsp garlic, chopped	400 g (14 oz) tin of chopped tomatoes
1 tbsp ginger, chopped	3 tbsp Thai red curry paste
1 small onion, chopped	peperonella sauce, to taste
1½ tbsp orange zest, finely chopped	2 tbsp tomato purée
6 rashers of bacon, rinded and chopped	4 tbsp olive oil
450 g (1 lb) minced beef	salt and freshly ground pepper
2 red peppers	fresh basil, chopped
2 yellow peppers	fresh chives, chopped
1 tbsp sugar	

Begin by cooking the noodles in salted water, according to the instructions on the packet. Heat the wok, and add the ginger, garlic and orange zest. Fry for 2 minutes before adding the onion. Cook until the onions are soft. Then add the minced beef and bacon which should be cooked until brown. Next add red and yellow peppers, tomatoes, tomato purée, sugar, peperonella sauce, curry paste, champagne, salt and pepper. Simmer for 30 minutes. Finally, drain the noodles and combine with the sauce. Garnish with plenty of basil and chives.

Cashew Nut and Vegetable Couscous

BRENDA TYSSEN, SOUTH YORKSHIRE

Serves 6 – 8

100 g (4 oz) cashew nuts	225 g (8 oz) courgettes, sliced
3 tbsp soy sauce	1 red pepper, diced
6 tbsp olive oil	225 g (8 oz) couscous
2 garlic cloves, crushed	225 g (8 oz) mushrooms, sliced
1 tsp curry powder	40 ml (1½ fl oz) white wine vinegar
2 tbsp tomato purée	fresh chopped parsley
1 vegetable stock cube	salt
350 ml (12 fl oz) water	freshly ground pepper

Pre-heat the oven to 190°C/375°F/Gas 5. Roast the cashew nuts in the oven until just golden. Then remove them from the oven and coat with the soy sauce.

Cover the bottom of a large pan with olive oil, add the garlic, curry powder and tomato purée.

Meanwhile, make up the vegetable stock. Pour the stock into the pan and bring to the boil. Add the courgettes and red pepper and cook for a further minute before adding the couscous. Then remove from the heat, cover and set aside.

Leave to stand for 10 minutes.

Meanwhile, cook the mushrooms in some olive oil and add them to the mixture along with the cashew nuts. Stir the couscous with a fork until it's fluffy. Finally, make a vinaigrette from the remaining olive oil and white wine vinegar. Season to taste and garnish with parsley.

Easy Savoury Rice

R. WILLIAMS, LINCOLNSHIRE

Serves 2

I tbsp olive oil	boiling water measured to 275 ml (10 fl oz) level in a measuring jug
I small onion, finely chopped	
rice measured to 150 ml (5 fl oz) level in a measuring jug	salt
	3 tbsp chives, chopped
a few strands of saffron or I tsp turmeric	

Heat oil in small saucepan. Gently fry the onion until soft. Add the rice and saffron or turmeric and stir to get the grains thoroughly coated.

Add the boiling water and a little salt and bring back to the boil. Cover immediately and simmer for 10 minutes without removing the lid. Remove the lid and leave, covered with a clean tea towel for 5–10 minutes.

Fluff up with a fork and add chives before serving.

Eddie Kidd's Chicken with Ginger & Spring Onion

STUNTMAN

Serves 4

2 large cloves garlic	2.5cm (I in) ginger root
8 tbsp soy sauce	50 g (2 oz) butter
I tsp lemon juice	450 g (I lb) rice
4 boneless chicken breasts	salt
6 spring onions	freshly ground pepper

Preheat the oven to 160°C/325°F/Gas 3.

Chop the garlic and put it into a bowl with the soy sauce, add the seasoning and lemon juice and leave to stand. Skin the chicken, thinly shred the spring onions lengthwise and chop the ginger into thin strips.

Grease some tin foil and then rub the remaining butter into the chicken breasts. Place the chicken on the foil, sprinkle it with a little ginger and the spring onions and pour over the soy sauce mixture. Season to taste. Fold the foil into a loose parcel and place in the oven for 45–50 minutes.

Boil the rice in plenty of salted water, then divide it between four plates. Place the chicken on it and pour the sauce over the top.

Marti Caine's Lotus White Chicken Fritters

SINGER, COMEDIENNE AND TV PERSONALITY

Serves 4

5 egg whites	pepper, to taste
120 ml (4 fl oz) chicken stock	4 chicken breasts (cooked or uncooked),
1 tsp dry sherry	skinned and finely chopped
1 tsp cornflour	oil for deep-frying
pinch of salt	

Place the egg whites in a large bowl but do not whisk or mix.

In a separate bowl, mix together the chicken stock, sherry, cornflour, salt and pepper, and add to the bowl of eggs. Add the chopped chicken to the bowl and stir the mixture.

Place 1 inch of oil in the bottom of a wok or deep frying pan and heat. The oil is hot enough when a cube of white bread, dropped in to test the heat, turns golden brown in 20 seconds.

Carefully place one ladleful of the mixture into the pan and watch it bubble and rise to the top of the pan. Turn it over and cook on the reverse side until it is golden and crisp. Remove from the pan with a slotted spoon and allow to drain on kitchen paper. Repeat until the remaining fritter mixture is used up.

Serve with a really tasty chutney and a crisp mixed salad.

Creamy Garlic Chicken

SALLY WEYMOUTH, WILTSHIRE

Serves 4

1 tbsp oil	½ glass dry white wine
4 chicken breasts, boned and skinned	125 g (4½ oz) garlic and herb
1 large onion, sliced	cream cheese
1 clove of garlic, crushed	salt and freshly ground black pepper
250 g (8 oz) mushrooms, sliced	250 g (8 oz) tagliatelle
1 leek, sliced	

Heat oil in a frying pan. Cut chicken into bite-sized pieces and brown slightly in the hot oil, then remove with a slotted spoon. Fry the onion, garlic and leek gently, until softened. Add the sliced mushrooms and continue to fry for 2 minutes.

Return chicken to the pan, add the wine and simmer for 5 minutes, stirring occasionally. Add the cheese and stir gently over low heat until it has melted. Add seasoning to taste.

Meanwhile, cook tagliatelle as directed on the packet. Combine with sauce and serve.

Barbecue Spare Ribs

DELLA STORR, SURREY

Serves 4

450 g (1 lb) pork spare ribs	3–4 tsp lemon juice
4 tbsp tomato ketchup	2 tsp hoisin sauce
1 tbsp black treacle	

Pre-heat the oven to 190°C/375°F/Gas 5.
Place spare ribs in a casserole dish with a lid. Put casserole dish in the oven for 45–50 minutes.

Towards the end of the cooking time, place the treacle, lemon juice and hoisin sauce in a sauce pan. Mix and heat through.

Remove the casserole dish from the oven and drain off the juices. Pour over the barbecue sauce and return the dish to the oven for a further 30 minutes, uncovered. Baste the ribs once during this time with the sauce.

Serve with jacket potatoes and a salad.

Red Lentil and Vegetable Curry

WENDY FRANCIS, CORNWALL

Serves 4

4 tsp oil	425 g (15 oz) can chopped tomatoes
1 onion, chopped	225 g (8 oz) split red lentils
2 cloves garlic, finely chopped	600 ml (1 pint) vegetable stock
175 g (6 oz) diced carrot	lemon juice
2 sticks celery, chopped	salt and pepper
4 tsp curry powder	

Heat oil and stir-fry onion and garlic for a few minutes. Add the carrot, celery and curry powder. Stir in tomatoes, lentils and stock and bring to the boil. Cover, reduce heat and simmer for 20-25 minutes, adding more stock if necessary. Season with lemon juice, salt and pepper.

DESSERTS

Linford Christie's
Apricot and Banana Crumble

ATHLETE

Serves 4

For the filling	For the crumble
395 g (14 oz) can apricot halves in fruit juice, drained	75 g (3 oz) butter, softened
	225 g (8 oz) plain flour
2 ripe bananas, chopped	75 g (3 oz) demerara sugar
4 tbsp water	pinch of ground mixed spice
1 tbsp clear honey	*To decorate*
	twists of lemon
	grated lemon rind
	mint leaves

Pre-heat the oven to 180°C/350°F/Gas 4. Place the apricots and banana pieces in an ovenproof dish, and pour the water and honey over them.

To make the crumble, cut the butter into small pieces. Place the flour in a large bowl and rub the butter into the flour with your fingertips until it resembles fine breadcrumbs. Fold in the sugar and mixed spice.

Spoon the topping over the fruit filling. Cook in the oven for 30 minutes or until golden. Decorate with the lemon pieces, grated lemon rind and mint leaves. Serve hot or cold with fat-free fromage frais.

Walnut Pie

MRS GERALDINE LANCASTER, WEST YORKSHIRE

Serves 6

For the pastry	For the filling
175 g (6 oz) plain flour	100 g (4 oz) butter
a pinch of salt	225 g (8 oz) soft brown sugar
cold water to mix	3 egg yolks
40 g (2 oz) lard, in small pieces	25 g (1 oz) plain flour
40 g (2 oz) butter or margarine	1 tsp vanilla essence
in small pieces	small tin evaporated milk
	100 g (4 oz) walnuts

Pre-heat the oven to 200°C/400°F/Gas 6. Place the flour and salt in a large bowl. Rub the fat into the flour until it resembles fresh breadcrumbs. Mix in enough cold water to bind. Put in a plastic bag and chill. Roll out the shortcrust pastry and use it to line the flan tin. Chill in the fridge. Meanwhile, cream the butter, sugar and egg yolks together until light and fluffy. Stir in the flour, vanilla essence and evaporated milk. Put the walnuts in a 20 cm (8 in) flan tin, and then pour over the prepared mixture. Bake in the oven for 10 minutes. Then reduce the heat to 140°C/275°F/Gas 1 and bake for a further 40 minutes or until the mixture has set. This dessert is delicious either hot or cold, and can be frozen.

Kate Robbins' Bun in the Oven

COMEDIENNE

Serves 4

250 ml (8 fl oz) fresh milk	2 tsp walnuts, chopped (optional)
200 g (7 oz) caster sugar	100 g (4 oz) sultanas
100 g (4 oz) butter	200 g (8 oz) plain flour
2 tsp mixed spice	3 tsp baking powder

Pre-heat the oven to 180°C/350°F/Gas 4. Place the milk, sugar and butter into a large pan. Add the mixed spice, walnuts (if using) and sultanas and simmer gently on a low heat, stirring all the time, until the mixture is smooth. Remove from the heat and allow to cool for 15 minutes. Whisk in the flour and the baking powder. Bring the mixture to a dough, starting with a wooden spoon and finishing with your hands. Shape into a round and place on a baking tray. Cook in the oven for 1 hour, until golden brown.

The Breakthrough Team's Favourite Chocolate Truffle Cake

Serves 6

750 g (1½ lb) plain chocolate	Cocoa for dusting
375 g (13 oz) unsalted butter	selection of berries to decorate
8 eggs	23 cm (9 in) springform tin, greased and lined with baking parchment

Pre-heat the oven to 200°C/400°F/Gas 6. Melt the chocolate and butter over a pan of simmering water and allow to cool. Separate the eggs and beat the whites until stiff peaks form. In a separate bowl, beat the egg yolks until creamy, then mix both whites and yolks together and beat well.

Gradually fold the melted chocolate and butter into the eggs by pouring it slowly down the side of the bowl. Fold the two mixtures together thoroughly until the chocolate mix becomes quite thick. Pour it into the tin and place in the middle of the oven. After 10 minutes, cover the tin with foil and cook for a further 10 minutes. Remove from the oven and allow to cool.

Remove the springform tin, retaining the base. Cover with foil and chill overnight. To serve, remove the foil, invert the cake onto a plate and carefully loosen the base of the tin with a knife. Peel off the baking parchment, dust the cake with the cocoa powder and decorate with berries.

Butterscotch Pudding

MRS ROSEMARY CARTWRIGHT, SURREY

Serves 3–4

6 oz soft brown sugar	2 eggs
3 oz margarine	½ tsp vanilla essence
4 oz self-raising flour	double cream, to serve

Pre-heat the oven to 180°C/350°F/Gas 4.

Melt the sugar and margarine together in a saucepan, then add the flour. Mix with a wooden spoon. In another bowl, beat the eggs well and add to the mixture. Cook for 1 minute in a saucepan, stirring all the time, then add the vanilla essence. Put into a well-greased tin and cook for 25 minutes. Turn it out into individual bowls and serve it warm with lashings of double cream.

Gary Rhodes'
Lemon and Lime Posset

CHEF AND COOKERY WRITER

Serves 6

900 ml (1½ pints) double cream	juice of 2 lemons
250 g (9 oz) caster sugar	juice of 2 limes

Boil the cream and sugar together in a saucepan for 2–3 minutes. Add the juice of the lemons and limes and mix well. Leave to cool slightly and then pour into six glasses and leave to set in the fridge.

This delicious dessert is even better when served with a little more cream poured on top.

The Rocking Horse
Blueberry Scone

MR RUHL, NORFOLK

Makes 20-24 scones

1 kg (2 lb) self-raising flour	150 g (5 oz) sugar
pinch of salt	350 g (12 oz) blueberries
225 g (8 oz) soft margarine or butter	450 ml (15 fl oz) milk

Pre-heat the oven to 200°C/400°F/Gas 6 and grease a large baking sheet.

Sift the flour and salt together into a large mixing bowl. Add the margarine and rub in with your fingers, until the mixture resembles fine breadcrumbs.

Add the sugar, the blueberries and the milk and mix together until you have a soft dough. If the dough is too wet, add a little more flour; if it is too dry, add a little more milk. Turn the dough out onto a floured board and roll to a thickness of 2 cm (¾ in). Using a 4-5 cm (1½-2 in) cutter (either fluted or plain), cut out as many scone shapes as you can (you should get at least 20).

Place the scones on the baking sheet and bake for 20-30 minutes or until lightly browned and firm to the touch. Cool and serve either cold or lukewarm with butter and blueberry jam.

Fern Britton's
Banana Rumbumble

TV PERSONALITY

Serves 4

4 bananas	**1 tbsp brandy**
100 g (4 oz) butter	**ice–cream or cream to serve**
50 g (2 oz) muscovado sugar	

Melt the butter in a large frying pan, add the bananas and fry until they begin to soften. Add the sugar and brandy and cook until the liquid bubbles. Serve immediately with ice–cream or cream.

Jo Brand's
Bread and Butter Pudding

COMEDIENNE

Serves 1 or 2

1 whole egg plus one yolk	**3-4 slices of bread, buttered**
50 g (2 oz) caster sugar	**50 g (2 oz) sultanas and raisins, mixed**
450 ml (15 fl oz) milk	**15 g (½ oz) candied peel**
drop of vanilla essence	

Pre-heat the oven to 180°C/350°F/Gas 4. Beat the egg with a tablespoon of the sugar. Bring the milk to boiling point, then pour it on to the egg mixture whisking all the time. Add the vanilla essence, whisk and leave to cool.

Butter an ovenproof dish and line it with a third of the bread slices. Sprinkle with dried fruit, then add another layer of bread. Add another layer of fruit, and a final layer of bread on the top. Pour over the custard and let it soak for a while before you bake it. Sprinkle the top with the remaining sugar and bake it for about 30 minutes.

Bread and Butter Pudding **is Gary Rhodes' signature dish but is Jo Brand more interested in her cakehole?**

Sophie Grigson's
Sweet Avocado Fritters

COOKERY WRITER

Serves 8

2 ripe avocados	2 eggs, separated
50 g (2 oz) caster sugar	120 ml (4 fl oz) water (approximately)
3 tbsp rum	1 tbsp oil
For the batter	oil for deep-frying
75 g (3 oz) plain flour	a little icing sugar, to serve
pinch of salt	wedges of lime, to serve
1 tbsp rum	

Halve and peel the avocados, removing the stones, then slice them thickly across the width to form crescents. Gently mix the slices with the caster sugar and rum.

To make the batter, sift the flour with the salt and make a well in the centre. Add the rum and egg yolks, then gradually mix in the water to give a smooth batter with the consistency of thickish single cream. Rest the mixture for 30 minutes. Just before using, whisk the egg whites until stiff. Add the oil to the batter and fold in the egg whites.

Heat the oil for deep-frying to about 195°C/385°F. Drain the avocado and dip each slice into the batter, coating evenly. Deep-fry until puffed and golden. Drain briefly on kitchen paper, dust with icing sugar and serve immediately with a squeeze of lime juice before the batter turns soggy.

Crunch Cream Pudding

WENDY PERRY, SURREY

Serves 4-6

4 Crunchie bars	300 ml (10 fl oz) whipping cream

Break the Crunchie bars into small pieces by putting them into a plastic bag and bashing them with a rolling-pin. Whip the cream until it stands in soft peaks. Fold in the Crunchie bar pieces, then divide between 6 serving glasses. Keep in the fridge until ready to serve.

Judi Spiers' Carrot Cake

TV PRESENTER

Serves 6-8

2 eggs	50 g (2oz) dessicated coconut
100 g (4 oz) dark brown sugar	2 tsp orange rind, grated
85 ml (3 fl oz) oil (sunflower or groundnut)	100 g (4 oz) walnuts, chopped
175 g (6 oz) carrots, finely grated	*For the icing*
100 g (4 oz) wholemeal self-raising flour	100 g (4½ oz) icing sugar
1 tsp ground cinnamon	Rind of ½ an orange plus 4 tsp orange juice
½ tsp allspice	(or rind and juice of one lemon)

Pre-heat the oven to 190°C/375°F/Gas 5. Grease and line the base of an 18cm (7 in) cake tin. In a large bowl, beat together the eggs and sugar until creamy. Very slowly, whisk in the oil. Gently fold in the grated carrots and the rest of the ingredients until well mixed. Pour into the cake tin and bake in the pre–heated oven for 25-30 minutes, until firm to the touch. Cool on a wire rack.

To make the icing: sift icing sugar into a bowl, add rind and juice and mix well. Spread over the cake.

Tony Blackburn's Mango Fool

RADIO PERSONALITY

Serves 8-10

450 g (1 lb) tin mango slices or about	6 cardamom heads, peeled and crushed
275g (10oz) of fresh, stoned, mango	10 g (¼ oz) caster sugar, to taste
200 ml (7 fl oz) evaporated milk	300ml (½ pint) whipping cream

Put the mango, evaporated milk and cardamom seeds into a food processor, and blend until smooth. Add the sugar if necessary. Whip cream and fold into mixture . Pour into a large serving bowl or individual dishes, and chill for 20 minutes. Serve with extra whipped cream, if liked.

Martyn Lewis's Daughter's Spiced Chocolate Chip Cookies

TV NEWSCASTER'S DAUGHTER

Makes 24

150 g (5 oz) self-raising flour	½ tsp ground mace
50 g (2 oz) granulated sugar	I egg
50 g (2 oz) soft brown sugar	100 g (4 oz) butter, cut into small cubes
½ tsp ground ginger	100 g (4 oz) good milk chocolate,
½ tsp ground nutmeg	coarsely chopped

Pre-heat the oven to 190°C/375°F/Gas 5. Grease two baking sheets.

In a food processor, mix the flour, sugars and spices for a few seconds. Add the egg and the butter and process for 5 seconds. Add the chocolate. Process the mixture for a further 5 seconds. With a teaspoon, place dollops onto the baking sheets, spreading them quite widely apart. Bake for 10–15 minutes. Leave to cool for 2 minutes and then serve warm. They should be hard on the outside and soft in the centre.

Apple Raspberry Crumble

LETA HARRIS, MIDDLESEX

Serves 4-6

For the filling	For the crumble
450 g (I lb) cooking apples, peeled and sliced	150 g (5 oz) plain flour
225 g (½ lb) raspberries, fresh or frozen	I tsp cinnamon
I½ tbsp brown sugar	50 g (2 oz) caster sugar
rind and juice of ½ an orange	75 g (3 oz) butter, diced
	23 cm (9 in) ovenproof dish

Pre-heat the oven to 190°C/375°F/Gas 5. Put the fruit into the dish, sprinkle with the brown sugar, orange rind and juice. Cook in the oven for 10 minutes. Remove and allow to cool.

Sieve the flour and cinnamon into a bowl and add the caster sugar. Rub in the butter until the mixture resembles fine breadcrumbs. Sprinkle it over the fruit and return to the oven for a further 35 minutes until the crumble is golden.

Anneka's Fruit Surprise

CREATED BY KEN HOM FOR ANNEKA RICE

3 heaped tbsp caster sugar	75 g (3 oz) blueberries
25 ml (7½ fl oz) water	250 g (9 oz) raspberries
2 tbsp butter	4 fresh basil leaves
250 g (9 oz) strawberries	

Dissolve the sugar in the water over a low heat, stirring continuously. Bring to the boil and simmer until a syrup has formed. Stir in the butter.

Add the strawberries, allow to warm through and then add the blueberries. Bring to simmering point and then add the raspberries. Add the basil leaves, and then simmer for 5–10 minutes or until the fruit is just soft.

Serve spooned over vanilla ice-cream in individual dishes.

Yoghurt Mousse with Orange Compote

ANNA TSPSCHISTOPOLSKA

Serves 4

150 g (5 oz) double cream	2 egg whites
150 g (5 oz) natural yoghurt	6 oranges
1 tsp vanilla essence	4 tsp icing sugar
2 tbsp caster sugar	2 tbsp orange liqueur

Whisk cream and then combine with the yoghurt. Add the sugar and vanilla and chill for half an hour. Whisk egg whites until stiff and fold into the yoghurt and cream mixture. Put back in the fridge.

Slice the tops and bottoms off the oranges and slide the blade of a knife between flesh and orange, cutting away all the pith. Retain the rind of 1 orange. Slice the flesh finely and sprinkle with icing sugar and orange liqueur. Blanch the retained orange rind for 1 minute in boiling water and scatter over the flesh, reserving a few strands for garnishing.

Divide the orange mixture between 4 glasses, top up with the mousse mixture and scatter with orange peel. Chill before serving.

Ian McCaskill's
Aunty Annie's Oaten Biscuits

TV WEATHERMAN'S AUNTY

Makes 24

100 g (4 oz) self-raising flour	75 g (3 oz) hard margarine
100 g (4 oz) medium oatmeal or porridge oats	3 tsp sugar
	1 egg, beaten
¼ tsp salt	

Pre-heat the oven to 180°C/350°F/Gas 4. Mix together the flour, oatmeal and salt. Rub in the margarine and add the sugar. Bind the dough with the egg and divide this mixture into two. Roll out the dough on a floured board and cut into biscuits with a 6 cm (2½ in) cutter. Place on a greased baking tray and cook for 15-20 minutes, until firm but not browned.

Ian McCaskill
takes the biscuit

Nan's Bakewell Tarts

MANDY CLEMENTS, HERTFORDSHIRE

Makes 10–12 tarts

225 g (½ lb) bought shortcrust pastry	a few drops of almond essence
25 g (1 oz) ground almonds	10–12 tsp jam
50 g (2 oz) caster sugar	*For the water icing*
2 tsp ground rice	4 tbsp icing sugar
1 egg	2 tbsp water

Pre-heat the oven to 190°C/375°F/Gas 5.

Roll out pastry, cut into rounds and use to line 10-12 patty tins. Mix the ground almonds, sugar, rice and egg yolk. Beat the white of egg till stiff and fold it into the mixture. Add the almond essence. Put a teaspoonful jam in the bottom of each pastry case and add the mixture to it. Cook in the oven for 25 minutes. Cool the tarts. Mix the icing sugar and water and brush over tarts.

Frozen Strawberry Pie

MRS NICKI ROUSE, NORTHAMPTON

Serves 4–6

175 g (6 oz) digestive biscuits, crushed	165 g (5½ oz) caster sugar
75 g (3 oz) margarine, melted	1 tbsp lemon juice
2 egg whites	300 ml (½ pint) whipping cream
275 g (10 oz) frozen strawberries	

Part defrost the strawberries.

Mix together the digestive biscuits and margarine and press into a 20 cm (8 in) greased flan tin, preferably loose bottomed.

Beat the egg whites until stiff, then add the strawberries, caster sugar and lemon juice and beat again. Whip the cream until softly peaked, fold into the strawberry mixture.

Make a greaseproof paper collar for the flan tin, to support any excess mixture. Pour the mixture into the flan tin and freeze for a few hours.

Remove from paper and flan tin while still frozen, defrost for 30–45 minutes before serving.

Mrs Solomon's Chocolate Cake

MRS SOLOMON, DEVON

Serves 8

150 g (5 oz) self-raising flour	3 size 1 eggs
175 g (6 oz) caster sugar	3 tbsp boiling water
175 g (6 oz) soft margarine	black cherry jam (optional)
75 g (3 oz) drinking chocolate	20-23 cm (8-9 in) cake tin, greased and lined

Pre-heat the oven to 180°C/350°F/Gas 4. Put all ingredients in a large mixing bowl and mix until well combined. Beat for two minutes, then transfer to the cake tin. Bake in the centre of the oven for about one hour until well risen.

Allow to cool in the tin for five minutes before transferring to a cooling rack. If desired, split in half and spread the centre with black cherry jam. Place melted chocolate or butter cream on top when completely cooled.

Lemon Crunch

MRS NICHOLS, KENT

Serves 4–6

275 g (10 oz) digestive biscuits	170 g (5¾ oz) tin condensed milk
100 g (4 oz) margarine	juice of 3 lemons
275 g (10 oz) double cream	

Crush the biscuits with a rolling pin. Melt the margarine and mix with the crushed biscuits. Use the biscuit mixture to form a base in a 23 cm (9 in) flan tin and put in the fridge to set. Whip the double cream until thick, add the condensed milk and whip again. Add the juice of the lemons and pour over the biscuit base. Leave to set in the fridge for a few hours before serving.

Tracy Edwards' Cupboard Chocolate Surprise

YACHTSWOMAN

Serves 4

2 medium-sized cans of sterilized cream	**I heaped tbsp white sugar**
5 heaped tbsp cocoa powder	**brandy or whisky, to taste**

Pour the sterilized cream into a bowl and add the cocoa powder, sugar and whisky or brandy. Whisk with an electric mixer until smooth and full of bubbles.

Pour the mixture into 4 ramekins or a serving bowl and leave in the fridge overnight. In the morning your chocolate pudding will have miraculously set into chocolate mousse!

Quick Raspberry and Banana Sorbet

SOPHIE FORGAN, MILTON KEYNES

Serves 4

I large or 2 small bananas	**25 g (8 oz) frozen raspberries**

Mix the ingredients in a food processor for 4–5 minutes, or until thoroughly blended. Transfer in to a plastic or glass bowl, cover and freeze for 30 minutes.

Apple and Lemon Pudding

MANDY COLLINS, DEVON

Serves 4–5

1 very large (or 2 medium) Bramley apples	50 g (2 oz) sultanas
1 lemon	pinch of salt
100 g (4 oz) self-raising flour	a little milk
100 g (4 oz) soft margarine	1 egg
150 g (5 oz) sugar	

Pre-heat the oven to 180°C/350°F/Gas 4.
Remove the rind and juice from the lemon and reserve. Peel, core and slice the apples into an ovenproof dish (approximately 1½-pint size). Sprinkle 25 g (1 oz) sugar and half the lemon juice over.

Cream the margarine and 100 g (4 oz) sugar, stir in the egg, sift the flour with the salt, and gradually add to the mixture. When it becomes too stiff add the remainder of the lemon juice and enough milk to form a slow dropping consistency. Stir in the rind of the lemon and the sultanas.

Put this mixture on top of the apples, smooth over and bake for about 20 minutes, or until the top is light brown and crunchy and feels springy to the touch.

Yoghurt Cake

HELEN BALLARD, NORTH HUMBERSIDE

Serves 8

100 g (4 oz) butter	3 eggs
225 g (8 oz) caster sugar	rind of ½ lemon, grated
150 g (5 oz) plain yoghurt	225 g (8 oz) plain flour, sifted

Pre-heat the oven to 180°C/350°F/Gas 4. Grease and line an 18 cm (7 in) cake tin with baking parchment.

Beat the butter and caster sugar together until pale and fluffy, then add the yoghurt and mix well. Slowly add the eggs, beating thoroughly. Add the grated lemon rind and fold in the flour.

Spread the smooth, thick batter into the prepared tin and bake for 1¼ hours.

Cumbrian Gingerbread

MRS NORMAN DIXON, CHESHIRE

Makes 2 × 450 g (1 lb) cakes

225 g (8 oz) lard	2 tsp mixed spice
225 g (8 oz) black treacle	2 large eggs
225 g (8 oz) soft brown sugar	300 ml (10 fl oz) milk
350 g (12 oz) plain flour	2 tsp bicarbonate of soda
2 tsp ground ginger	

Pre-heat the oven to 150°C/300°F/Gas 2. Line two 450 g (1 lb) loaf tins with baking parchment or greaseproof paper.

Slowly melt the lard, treacle and sugar in a heavy pan. Sift together the flour and spices in a large mixing bowl. Add the warm mixture and eggs to the flour and spices and mix well.

Warm the milk in a pan and stir in the bicarbonate of soda. Add to the mixture and stir well.

Divide the mixture equally between the two loaf tins and bake in the oven for 1¼–1½ hours or until firm to the touch. Leave to cool in the tins.

Chocolate Crisp Fudge

TRACY IRISH, HERTFORDSHIRE

Makes 12 pieces

125 g (5 oz) butter	200 g (7 oz) plain chocolate
5 Mars bars	25 g (1 oz) butter
125 g (5 oz) puffed rice cereal	

Lightly grease large glass dish. Melt the butter and Mars Bars gently in a saucepan and stir in the puffed rice. Spread into the dish and level out top.

Melt the chocolate and the remaining 25 g butter together and pour over puffed rice cereal. Place in the fridge overnight to harden then cut into pieces to serve.